THE
BIBLE
RECAP
DISCUSSION
GUIDE

Also by Tara-Leigh Cobble

THE
BIBLE
RECAP
DISCUSSION GUIDE

Weekly Questions for
Group Conversation on
THE ENTIRE BIBLE

TARA-LEIGH COBBLE

BETHANYHOUSE
a division of Baker Publishing Group
Minneapolis, Minnesota

© 2022 by Tara-Leigh Cobble

Published by Bethany House Publishers
Minneapolis, Minnesota
www.bethanyhouse.com

Bethany House Publishers is a division of
Baker Publishing Group, Grand Rapids, Michigan

Printed in the United States of America

Library of Congress Cataloging-in-Publication Data
Names: Cobble, Tara-Leigh, author.
Title: The Bible recap discussion guide : weekly questions for group conversation on the entire
    Bible / Tara-Leigh Cobble.
Description: Minneapolis, Minnesota : Bethany House Publishers, a division of Baker Publishing
    Group, [2022]
Identifiers: LCCN 2022022023 | ISBN 9780764241482 (paper) | ISBN 9781493442256 (ebook)
Subjects: LCSH: Bible—Examinations, questions, etc. | Cobble, Tara-Leigh. Bible recap.
Classification: LCC BS612 .C559 2022 | DDC 220.071—dc23/eng/20220621
LC record available at https://lccn.loc.gov/2022022023

Cover design by Rob Williams, InsideOut Creative Arts, Inc.

The author is represented by Alive Literary Agency, www.aliveliterary.com

Baker Publishing Group publications use paper produced from sustainable forestry practices and post-consumer waste whenever possible.

23 24 25 26 27 28 29   8 7 6 5 4 3

Contents

How to Use This Guide and Other Tools

First, please visit thebiblerecap.com/start. It will tell you all you need to know to join our reading plan and podcast. Then, we recommend doing the following steps each day, in this order:

1. Do your daily Bible reading according to The Bible Recap reading plan you've chosen: whole Bible (Old Testament and New Testament) or New Testament only.
2. Use *The Bible Recap Journal* during your reading (optional).
3. Use the daily *The Bible Recap Study Guide* after, or during, your reading (optional). We've left room underneath the questions where you can write your answers in the guide itself.
4. Listen to the corresponding podcast episode or read the entry in *The Bible Recap* book for more information, insights, and answers.
5. Use this book, *The Bible Recap Discussion Guide*, in group conversations about that week's reading plan. Since these questions are intended for group discussion, we did not aim to create space for answering in the guide itself.

The journal is intended to be self-guided, while the daily and weekly guides offer a higher level of challenge and connection. You don't have to have both guides (*The Bible Recap Study Guide* and *The Bible Recap*

Discussion Guide), but we created them to complement each other. The daily study guide questions tend to focus more on research and study, whereas the weekly discussion guide questions are more reflective and suited for personal discussion. If anyone in your discussion group is also using the journal or daily study guide, it can help further your conversation to ask for their input from what they've learned there.

This guide will occasionally reference your "God Shot"—a phrase used throughout *The Bible Recap* book and podcast. This term points to any "snapshot" you see of God's character or attributes from that day's reading.

In order to connect with and challenge all types of readers, we've offered a variety of questions throughout this guide—objective, subjective, critical thinking, as well as questions to help you sharpen your research skills. For those questions in the latter category, we've listed some tools below that you may find helpful.

Helpful Resources

Here are some free resources we've used in researching and writing this study and podcast. You may also find it helpful to purchase a physical copy of a study Bible or commentary. Some of our current favorites for broad use are the ESV Study Bible, *Matthew Henry's Commentary on the Whole Bible*, the Arthur W. Pink commentaries, and the Douglas J. Moo commentaries.

- **Study Bible:** bible.faithlife.com
- **Commentaries:** biblestudytools.com
- **Hebrew/Greek lexicon:** blueletterbible.org
- **Other websites:** bibleproject.com, gotquestions.org, biblecharts .org, desiringgod.org

While we can't offer a blanket endorsement of everything produced by these sites and resources (especially as content may change over time), we generally find them to be trustworthy and helpful.

Before you read God's Word each day, seek His help with these five prayers:

1. God, give me wisdom, knowledge, and understanding.

2. God, let any knowledge I gain serve to help me love You and others more, and not puff me up.

3. God, help me see something new about You I've never seen before.

4. God, correct any lies I believe about You or anything I misunderstand.

5. God, direct my steps according to Your Word.

1. Why do you think God gave us two separate accounts of creation (Genesis 1 and Genesis 2)?

2. Assuming we agree that God is the Creator of all things, do you view the creation narrative as literal, allegorical, or a general reductive summary? How—if at all—would your faith be impacted if you found out you were wrong in that particular view and that one of the other views was accurate instead?

3. How does it feel to be pursued by God in the midst of your sin? Scary? Comforting? Threatening? And why?

4. What's your perspective on the "sons of God" in Genesis 6?

5. *Optional (read if you have the study guide):* Revisit questions 1–3 from Day 3. Why is it important for us to notice whom specific commands and promises are given to? How have you seen commands or promises misapplied to people they aren't given to?

6. Does suffering confuse you like it does Job? How can you tell if you're being punished or disciplined by God, you're experiencing

an attack of the enemy, or it's just a natural part of life's hard circumstances?

7. Job believes God is ultimately sovereign over both his troubles and his hope. Are these things hard to reconcile? Why or why not?

8. Do you find it challenging to sit in silence with people in their pain? Are you inclined to try to fix the problem? What approach do you appreciate most in your own life?

9. What is your favorite thing you read about God's character in your God Shots from this week?

DAYS 8–14

1. In Job 4:12–16, Eliphaz claims his words of counsel come from a spirit. In 20:3, Zophar makes the same claim. Is it safe to assume all guidance and promptings we get are from God? How can we know what's true? Do you have any personal experiences with this?

2. Describe a time when you were obedient to God and things didn't work out like you wanted them to. Did you feel like God wasn't holding up His end of the agreement? What lies are at the root of this misguided belief? How did you come to understand the truth?

3. "Why do bad things happen to good people?" is a common question. Romans 3:10–12 says no human is good; so although Job isn't inherently good, God declares him righteous—ultimately, because of what Jesus did on the cross. Still, terrible things happen to him. In response to that question, "Why do bad things happen to good people?" R. C. Sproul Jr. said, "That only happened once, and He volunteered."* What do you think he meant by this response?

*Paul Derry and R. C. Sproul Jr., *Call Me Barabbas* (Inner Sanctum Publishing, Inc., 2020), 12.

4. In Job 33:19–30, Elihu says God sometimes allows people to struggle through trials and consequences in order to produce repentance in them. Describe a time when you've been in that situation.

5. A quote often attributed to Charles Spurgeon says, "I have learned to kiss the wave that strikes me against the Rock of Ages." Are you grateful for the way God used that trial to draw you nearer to Himself (even if you aren't grateful for the trial itself)? If so, how long did it take you to feel that gratitude?

6. Have you ever used pain as an excuse to sin, like Elihu suggests in Job 36:21?

7. When God finally speaks to Job, He doesn't answer any of Job's questions. He simply reminds Job that He is God. Imagine you're Job; would this feel like a comfort or a rebuke? Why?

8. What is your favorite thing you read about God's character in your God Shots from this week?

1. When God speaks, Job's tone and perspective shift. What does God say or reveal to Job that leads to that shift in attitude?

2. Do all the promises of God's covenant with Abram sound easy and desirable (Genesis 15)?

3. How, if at all, has your understanding of angels been reshaped by what we've read in Genesis so far?

4. How is circumcision a fitting symbol for God's people, the Israelites? How might that particular mark serve as a form of protection to keep them from sin?

5. Abraham has a lengthy negotiation with God where God willingly and patiently listens to Abraham's pleas. In the end, what ultimately changes from God's original plan? What might this reveal about human perspectives and limitations?

6. Read 2 Peter 2:7 aloud. How could Lot be declared righteous?

7. Much is said of Abraham's faith in offering Isaac as a sacrifice, but given Isaac's age, he certainly knows what's happening. How does Isaac portray Christ to us in this moment?

8. What do you think God might be revealing about Himself by denying Esau, the older brother, the position of honor and assigning it to Jacob, the younger brother, instead?

9. Later in Scripture, God begins to refer to Himself as the God of Abraham, Isaac, and Jacob. But at this point in the story, when He's talking with Isaac, He refers to Himself as the God of Abraham and Isaac. What does this seem to indicate about God? Is He the God of all people? If not, does that contradict His position as the One True God, Most High God, or God Over All?

10. What is your favorite thing you read about God's character in your God Shots from this week?

DAYS 22–28

1. As we studied the sins of Jacob and Laban, and Rachel and Leah, did you find any of their stories resonating with you? If so, how? Where have you seen God's patience and goodness to you in the midst of your story?

2. How can we discern which stories in Scripture are *descriptive* (like in Genesis 35) versus which are *prescriptive*?

3. After God renames Jacob "Israel," he is still regularly called by his old name, unlike what we saw with Abraham and Sarah. Why do you think that is?

4. What significant event happens in Jacob's life that signals the change when he starts replacing pillars with altars and referring to God by His name? Why is this meaningful?

5. What does the story of Judah and Tamar reveal to us about God?

6. Which part of Joseph's story was most heartbreaking for you? The family betrayal? The lies he endures from the person in power? The forgetful friend? Moses (the author of this passage) continues to remind us that God is with Joseph in all of this, yet his life is far

from easy. Have you ever felt like God left you alone in your pain? Did Joseph's story comfort you? Why or why not?

7. Egypt is blessed as a result of Joseph's presence during the famine. What does it reveal about God's heart that He uses one of His children to bless those outside His family?

8. In what ways do Joseph's brothers demonstrate that they are repentant and that their hearts have changed since they sold him into slavery?

9. What is your favorite thing you read about God's character in your God Shots from this week?

1. What do you think God is demonstrating by repeatedly foregoing the societal norm of primogeniture, where the oldest son gets the blessing? Does this seem fair? Why or why not?

2. Recalling Abraham's lies about Sarah and Isaac's lie about Rebekah, how are the lies of the Hebrew midwives different? What does this reveal about God?

3. God shows up to Moses and gives him an assignment *after* he had murdered someone. How would you feel if your pastor or boss had murdered someone before they became your leader? How do you think that incident would impact them and their view on their ability to lead?

4. *Optional (read if you believe it will benefit your group's conversation and not cause division):* In Exodus 4:21 and 7:3, God warns Moses about what will happen when he speaks to Pharaoh: God will harden Pharaoh's heart. These are hard verses to wrestle with, but try to think through some of the implications together: If God did this, was it fair? Why or why not? What does Pharaoh deserve? It's okay to wrestle with this question internally. If you choose to discuss this, aim to respect the viewpoints of others and where they are in their understanding of God and Scripture.

5. The Israelites don't believe God's promises because of their broken spirits and harsh circumstances. Can you relate? How has God proven Himself to be kinder than you had the faith to believe or hope for?

6. What can we learn from God's distinct treatment of the Israelites who doubt Him, the Egyptian servants who fear Him, and the Egyptians who don't fear Him?

7. Much like Christians look back to the resurrection of Christ for hope, Jewish people throughout history have looked back to the Exodus and to Passover for hope. Just as Christians celebrate Easter annually, Jews celebrate Passover annually. In fact, the timeline for the annual events overlaps. (Read 1 Corinthians 5:7 and Mark 14:1 aloud.) In the Passover story, how do we see God setting the stage for His people to understand the significance of Jesus's death?

8. God gave the Israelites instructions for how to celebrate and remember Him and His goodness to them, whether times were good or bad. When are you most likely to forget God? In struggle and lack? Or in abundance and ease?

9. Some of the Israelites disobeyed God's commands for the Sabbath by gathering manna on that day. From their actions, what can we discern about their beliefs about God?

10. What is your favorite thing you read about God's character in your God Shots from this week?

DAYS 36–42

1. How would you describe "the fear of the Lord"? How is the fear of the Lord different for those who know Him versus those who don't?

2. God is equipping the Israelites with the most basic information they need to establish a civil society. He'll continue to add to these laws throughout their time in the wilderness, giving them a series of instructions and commands. In fact, there are 613 commands throughout the Torah (the first five books of the Bible). What seems distinct about the Ten Commandments? Why do they seem to fall into their own category?

3. Is God's attention to detail in all the tabernacle descriptions comforting? Why or why not?

4. What differences did you notice between how the world portrays cherubim and how Scripture describes them?

5. Read Hebrews 9:22 aloud. While the sacrificial system is hard to stomach, the podcast reminds us that we should never be angrier at the provision for sin than at the sin itself. Is this a struggle for you? Why or why not?

6. How does Bezalel's work in Exodus 31:1–11 vary from Aaron's work in 32:1–5? Why is one God-honoring and one sinful?

7. Most product packaging lists ingredients in the order of quantity, meaning the first product in the list is the most prominent, and the last product is the least prominent. With that in mind, read Exodus 34:6–7 aloud and discuss how this could potentially apply.

8. Repeatedly, chapter 35 says tabernacle donations are made by everyone whose heart stirs them up or moves them. How do hearts get stirred and moved? How does that change happen?

9. What is your favorite thing you read about God's character in your God Shots from this week?

1. Does the sacrificial system trouble you? Why or why not?

2. Knowing that our sins are treason against the kingdom of God, and that blood must be shed to cover our sins (Hebrews 9:22), can you think of a different solution to this problem?

3. How would you describe the differences between being unclean, being clean, and being holy? Give at least one example of each.

4. There are very strict laws surrounding the presence of God and regarding it with humility, yet sinful people are called to bring their offerings and sacrifices *to* Him, not to make them outside the camp. What does this reveal about God's heart toward sinners? What is God's relationship to the presence of sin?

5. When God gives detailed instructions about what to eat, what not to eat, and how to deal with skin diseases and household mold, does it feel more controlling or loving to you? Why might the Israelites need to hear these instructions?

6. In Leviticus 14:34, God takes responsibility for being sovereign over the (hypothetical) leprous condition of the house. Is it

comforting to know God is in control of those things? If not, who do you think should be, or is, in control of them? Why?

7. In 17:7, God says the people have been making sacrifices to "goat demons." Do you think the people know they're sacrificing to demons and don't care? Are they deceived by the enemy? What do you think is the most likely scenario? Why?

8. What is your favorite thing you read about God's character in your God Shots from this week?

1. How would you summarize the three basic types of laws: civil laws, ceremonial laws, and moral laws?

2. How can we discern which types of laws are being given in Scripture? Which laws still apply?

3. As far as God's covenant with the Israelites is concerned, He promises discipline when they rebel. How is discipline different from punishment—in motive, attitude, and goal?

4. How do we rightly view wrath, punishment, discipline, and consequences for our sins in light of Christ's death on the cross? Aim to root your answers in Scripture (likely from the New Testament). See Romans 8:1 for help.

5. How is God's wrath expressed toward those who don't know Him and submit to Jesus as Lord? Aim to root your answers in Scripture (likely from the New Testament). See John 3:36 for help.

6. God chooses the Levites to be the tribe that serves Him in the tabernacle. He also appoints the division of labor between the three clans of the Levites. Do you think this appointment caused strife

between tribes or clans? Why do you think God may have chosen to work this way?

7. Why might God have given rules on how to address suspected adultery instead of only giving laws for proven or known adultery?

8. What is your favorite thing you read about God's character in your God Shots from this week?

DAYS 57–63

1. How is the people's grumbling to each other about their circumstances different from Moses' complaining to God about the people?

2. It's likely that Miriam and Aaron are some of the people whom God speaks through in Numbers 11:25. How might that have contributed to their arrogance in 12:2?

3. If we consider the ancient Jewish view that the Nephilim from Genesis 6 were destroyed in the flood, how is it possible that they could be living in Canaan when the spies arrive?

4. Looking back over the past few books, describe the trajectory of the Israelites' attitude since they came into the wilderness. What traits have you seen them display?

5. When the ten spies report that Israel can't take the land, Israel believes them instead of God. Then God promises a consequence for their sins. Essentially, they will get exactly what they believed and asked for: They won't get to dwell in the land, and they'll die in the desert instead. When God tells them this, they try to take the land. What seems to be motivating their actions? Are they suddenly faith filled? Are they repentant? Fearful?

6. Korah leads 250 people in a rebellion against Moses. Ultimately, why are they rebelling?

7. Moses rebels against God by striking the rock in front of all the people, instead of speaking to it as God commanded. As a result, he doesn't get to enter the promised land. Why do you think Moses is held to a higher standard with his obedience? Is there anything else that might also factor in here? (See Numbers 14:29–35 if you need help.)

8. What do you think motivates Balaam in his actions toward Israel and King Balak?

9. What is your favorite thing you read about God's character in your God Shots from this week?

1. The words we use are important and significant, but Balaam knows that his words are worthless against God's plan; he can't curse people God has blessed. How does this idea compare to the common belief that we have the power to speak things into existence? Can you think of a time when you've been tempted to ascribe too much power to your own words? Or to someone else's?

2. Moses has pushed back regularly on some of God's declarations about what He's going to do. Does he ever push back on God's decision that he won't enter the promised land? Why do you think he responds to this the way he does?

3. Why do you think God needs to keep reminding people to worship only Him and to rest? How are those two commandments connected?

4. Which commandments are the most difficult for you to keep?

5. Why is God so adamant that the Israelites drive out all the Canaanites in the promised land?

6. Is the distinction between "murderer" and "manslayer" in Numbers 35 a challenging one for you? Why or why not?

7. What does it reveal about God's character that He protects specific plots of land for the descendants of Esau and Lot, even though they aren't among the tribes of Israel? Does Scripture give us any indication of why He does this?

8. What is your favorite thing you read about God's character in your God Shots from this week?

1. The Transjordan tribes (Reuben, Gad, half of Manasseh) ask for land east of the Jordan River that is not part of the original land God promised to the Israelites, and God gives it to them. What does this reveal about God's heart? Since this land isn't part of the original covenant, does it or should it have the same promises attached to it?

2. Why does God need to give a refresher on all the laws to the people entering into the promised land?

3. Moses gives three warnings to the Israelites about the thoughts they may be tempted to have (Deuteronomy 7:17–18; 8:17–18; and 9:4). Which of these types of thoughts are you most prone to having? What truths from Scripture help you fight those lies when they creep into your mind?

4. The punishment for a false prophet in ancient Israel is death. Why do you think it's important for their laws about this to be strict? Can we know if someone is a false prophet? How?

5. The rabbis have a tendency to "build a fence around the law" but then treat the man-made "fence" like it's the God-given law. Can you think of any parallels to this in modern Christendom?

6. It's vital for the Israelites to live differently from the pagan Canaanites in the promised land—not worshipping or grieving in the ways they do, through cutting themselves and shaving their heads. Is it important for us to consider these types of things today? Why or why not?

7. What do you think God intends by commanding the Israelites to "purge the evil" from their midst? How is this similar to and different from Paul's use of the phrase in 1 Corinthians 5:13? And why are both important?

8. Is it frustrating that God has only given them basic laws for a civil society? Why do you think He hasn't given them laws that represent the full standard of holiness and righteousness?

9. What is your favorite thing you read about God's character in your God Shots from this week?

1. In Deuteronomy 28–30, God lays out the blessings and curses for the covenant He is entering into with the Israelites. Why is it important for us not to take these verses out of context and apply them today? What should we be looking for when we read these verses that does still apply today?

2. What purpose, or purposes, do the curses in the covenant agreement serve?

3. Read Deuteronomy 29:29 aloud. Is this verse comforting or frustrating to you? Why?

4. In Deuteronomy 31:17, God says the Israelites will blame their troubles on His absence instead of recognizing sin as the source of the problem. Have you ever falsely accused God for your trials?

5. Are you more inclined to rebel against God during times of trouble or in times of blessing? Why?

6. In Deuteronomy 32:21, God reveals another phase of His multi-step process to bring restoration in His relationship with humanity. He makes a promise to pursue the Gentiles (non-Jews) as a

part of His plan to draw Israel back to Himself someday. How does this process help reveal and clarify the distinction between Israel (the nation of people) and the church?

7. As the Israelites enter the promised land, God establishes celebrations for some significant days and events that were connected to the exodus (e.g., crossing dry land where He'd parted waters, the tenth day of the month of Nisan). Through this repetition, what truths do you think God is trying to reveal and reinforce about His character and His plan?

8. Achan's sin results in Israel losing the battle against Ai. What does this reveal about how God views and treats Israel? What aspects of this, if any, can be applied to the church today?

9. In our reading this week, God uses a lot of strange tactics in warfare: trumpets, torches, hail, panic, and cosmic phenomena. What does this reveal about God's power and how He works?

10. What is your favorite thing you read about God's character in your God Shots from this week?

1. Did you learn anything new about the location or layout of Israel through our study of tribal allotments this week? If so, what was it?

2. In the dispute over the altar at the border, the western tribes and the Transjordan tribes each have their own perspective on what the altar means. They're able to resolve the misunderstanding and keep the peace through reasoning and humility. Can you think of a time when you misunderstood someone else's motives or wrongly accused them?

3. Read Judges 2:10 aloud. One of Israel's problems is that they failed to teach their children the truth about God. As the older generation dies off, the younger generation is lured in by the ways of the Canaanites. Think of a time when you forgot the truth about God and your heart was lured in by the world. What lies were you believing about God that led you astray?

4. God repeatedly warned the Israelites about what would happen if they didn't drive out the Canaanites. As He begins fulfilling that promise, they fall into a cycle of repentance and rebellion. Why is it so hard to obey God even when we know the outcome of disobedience will be disastrous?

5. Deborah the prophetess is the only judge in Israel who fully honors God and the one who follows His commands most closely. Given her heart to follow Him, why isn't she the one appointed to lead Israel into battle? What traits of a good leader are demonstrated in her relationship with Barak?

6. Read Judges 6:12–13 aloud. Have you ever felt like this? Have you ever questioned God's presence or work in your life when things weren't going as you'd hoped? What did you learn through that experience? What does Gideon learn through his experience?

7. Gideon is trepidatious about following God's lead and asks for repeated confirmation. Is this the same thing as testing God? Why or why not?

8. God reduces Gideon's army to increase God's glory. What aspects of God's character do we see displayed through His process of narrowing down the army in Judges 7:2–10?

9. What is your favorite thing you read about God's character in your God Shots from this week?

1. Gideon is fearful but obedient, then he grows arrogant and wicked. What do you think prompts these changes in him? Which parts of his story resonated with you most? Why?

2. Read Judges 9:22–25 aloud. God takes credit for sending an evil spirit between wicked "King" Abimelech and the leaders of his town, Shechem. Now read 9:56–57. What does this story reveal to us about God? Is this comforting or offensive to you? Why?

3. In Judges 10, when the Israelites cry out to God for help, He tells them to seek help from the gods they've been worshipping instead. What prompts Him to change His response? (See 10:10–16 for help.) What does this reveal about Him?

4. Jephthah's story is a cautionary tale about the tragic consequences of misunderstanding God's Word. While we can hope he didn't actually follow through with sacrificing his daughter, we've likely all followed through on our own misunderstanding of Scripture at some point. Can you think of a time when you fervently followed counsel you thought was from God's Word but later found out wasn't?

5. Samson seems to believe his strength is in his long hair, but where does the text say his power comes from? How does it damage our view of God to take credit for our giftings?

6. Micah wants the appearance of godliness, but it's merely a path to power and control. The Danites have the same issue. Do you think they believe they're doing the right thing, or do they know better? Have you ever aimed for things that appeared godly but were actually self-exalting?

7. The story of the Levite and his concubine is gruesome and horrific. The wicked murder of one woman leads to the death of thousands in retaliation via Israel's first civil war, which God authorizes. What does this reveal about God's hatred of evil and His heart for justice and righteousness?

8. Read Judges 21:25 aloud. How do you see this playing out in your life today? Where do you do what you want without consulting God? What does the world look like when everyone does that?

9. What did we learn about God from seeing His response to Ruth's faith and Naomi's despair?

10. What is your favorite thing you read about God's character in your God Shots from this week?

1. The presence of God's earthly throne—the ark of the covenant—doesn't bring the Philistines the blessing they hoped it would. Later, we'll see that the people in an Israelite home where the ark is relocated are blessed by its presence (2 Samuel 6:10–12). What do these events reveal about the correlation between God, His presence, His blessings, and His children?

2. Why do you think God appoints a Benjamite as the first king of Israel? What function, or functions, might this serve given Israel's recent history with that tribe?

3. Where does Saul go wrong in his leadership? Did we see any signs beforehand that he would not make a good king? Why do you think God appointed this man to be Israel's first king?

4. What does the phrase "a man after God's own heart" (see 1 Samuel 13:14) mean? Does this mean David is perfect or that God approves of all of David's actions?

5. We saw lots of changes in Saul based on the presence of the Holy Spirit or the evil spirit that taunts him. We saw the evil spirit flee when David worshipped God. What are some things this reveals

or demonstrates about God's Spirit and His authority over evil? Is this comforting? Why or why not?

6. Read Psalm 18:19 and Zephaniah 3:17 aloud. God demonstrates His joy and delight in His children all throughout Scripture. This week we saw that the only time Scripture records God laughing is when He laughs *at His enemies* (Psalm 59:8, 2:4, and 37:12). How do these two things work in tandem? How do they display a fuller picture of God's character and emotions?

7. Read David's words in 1 Samuel 22:23 aloud. Saul and his men accuse David of "hiding" from him (23:18, 23), but David knows he's safe because of God's promises to him about being king. Saul tries to paint him in a negative light, but David is being faithful and following God's directives. Compare and contrast Saul's fear and David's faith, especially in light of Saul's power and David's vulnerability. What aspect of this encourages or challenges you?

8. David is God's appointed man for the throne. Why do you think God allows him to suffer through so many trials and attacks on his life? What do you think he learns about God in that process that he might not have known otherwise? Have you ever been through something similar?

9. What is your favorite thing you read about God's character in your God Shots from this week?

1. It's easy for us to want to be the source of God's vengeance toward our enemies, instead of trusting Him to act with perfect justice in the grand scheme of things. Read Psalm 35:11–14 aloud, then read 35:22–26 aloud. How does David respond to his enemies personally, and how does David ask God to respond to them? What does this reveal about David's view of God?

2. What's wrong with Saul seeking guidance from a medium? What does this reveal about his view of God? What does it reveal about his need for control and a sense of certainty?

3. In 1 Samuel 30, David has six hundred men following him. Of those, two hundred are too tired to go fight against the Amalekites. He and the four hundred others win the battle, but many of those who went with David are described as "wicked and worthless" and their actions are selfish and greedy. Read Luke 10:38–42 aloud. Compare and contrast these two sets of men with Mary and Martha. Discuss the distinction between actions and motives.

4. When David shows generosity to the two hundred who were too tired to fight, it points us back to Jesus and His generosity toward all of us—who have done nothing to earn the spoils of a battle we

didn't fight. Can you think of any other stories or parables from the life of Jesus that point to this reality?

5. This week we looked at the dangers of taking the promises in chapters like Psalm 128 and claiming them for ourselves. How has reading God's story in chronological order helped you grow and develop your understanding of which kinds of verses are specific and which kinds are general?

6. Read Psalm 130:4 aloud. How has your understanding of the fear of the Lord changed as we've moved through Scripture together?

7. With David as king of Judah, the largest tribe, and Ish-bosheth as king of all the remaining tribes, David is still waiting to officially be the king of Israel. Why do you think God didn't completely fulfill this promise the moment Saul died? What do we see happening in the waiting and the process?

8. Psalm 8:3–6 speaks of how unique mankind is among all God's creation and how He has crowned us with glory and honor. Then Psalm 14:1–3 (and Romans 3:10–12) point out that none are righteous and no one seeks God. How can these two ideas coexist in the fullness of truth?

9. What is your favorite thing you read about God's character in your God Shots from this week?

DAYS 113–119

1. What does it reveal about God that He gives us glimpses of the stories of Nimrod, Peleg, and Achan in the genealogies of 1 Chronicles 1–2?

2. David repeatedly "preaches the gospel to himself" in the Psalms, reminding himself of the truth of God's goodness amid all his trials. How often do your thoughts and emotions lie to you? How often do you need to be reminded of the truth? Have you made this a part of your regular prayer life or thought life? If so, what does that look like?

3. The tribes of Reuben, Simeon, and Levi were all impacted by the sins of their namesakes. Reuben slept with his father's concubine, and Simeon and Levi plotted and killed all the men of Shechem. In Scripture, God often regards groups of His own people as a *whole*, but since our modern, highly individualistic society favors the notion of personal rights and responsibilities, it's easy to view God's actions in a negative light. What are some of the positive implications of the way God's people are often regarded as a whole?

4. In Psalm 73 and Psalm 78, Asaph gives us two examples of what it's like to have a change in perspective. When his focus is on

himself or others, he grows bitter toward God. When his focus is on God and His goodness, he is humbled and repents. How have you seen this kind of transition play out in your own life? Can you think of a recent time when your mind was renewed?

5. Knowing that the Israelites will eventually go into exile, is it easier or harder for you to watch them wander off into sin repeatedly? Does it make it easier knowing God will bring them back to the land eventually? Would your perspective change if you were the one they were sinning against? Why or why not?

6. Read Psalm 92:1–2 aloud. The psalmist says it's good to bookend our days with praise. What are some ways you've incorporated the practice of praise into your days? What are some new things you're excited to try?

7. In Scripture, we see three accounts of Saul's death, which include two different versions of how it happened—one told by the authors of Scripture in 1 Samuel 31:3–6 and 1 Chronicles 10:3–6, and one told by the Amalekite sojourner in 2 Samuel 1:6–10. Out of context, these accounts seem to contradict each other. How does the inclusion of all three stories help us understand the truth and teach us the importance of reading in context?

8. What is your favorite thing you read about God's character in your God Shots from this week?

DAYS 120–126

1. In what area of his life does David seek God's direction? In what area of his life does David not seek God's direction and ignore His commands? In what ways do we tend to live similarly? Are there any areas of your life where you don't seek God's guidance?

2. First Chronicles 12:18, 33, and 38 reiterate that David's men had a singleness of purpose and all Israel was of a single mind to make David king. Given the division that existed during and after the reign of Saul, what do you think contributed to this new unity of the nation of Israel?

3. One of God's forms of discipline or punishment in Psalm 107:40 is to make people wander in trackless wastes. This creates a challenge for the helpless wanderer who has no path to follow and no idea how to move forward. In general, what kind of guidance does God offer His people? Is He making a way and showing them where to go, or is He leaving them to their own devices without a clear path? In what areas are you tempted to abandon His path to wander in your own wasteland?

4. The Philistines transported the ark on an oxcart, and David follows suit. During David's attempt, Uzzah touches the ark and dies. Hypothetically speaking, if the Philistines had to personally

position the ark on the oxcart, why aren't they held to the same standards of obedience as the Israelites? Would that display God's mercy to the Philistines, His discipline to Israel, or both?

5. Given the fact that psalms were once referenced by their first line, has your view of why Jesus quoted Psalm 22:1 on the cross changed your perspective of what happened there between the Father and the Son? Why or why not? Has it impacted the way you relate to the Father or the Son?

6. What are some green pastures and still waters God has brought you to lately? How has He nourished you and refreshed your soul? Did you resist it at first? Did He have to "make you" lie down?

7. Has it been challenging or encouraging (or both) to look at the Psalms with a lens to understand which parts are sharing facts about God and which parts are sharing feelings about God in light of the psalmist's circumstances? Is it hard for you to do this in your own life?

8. Is it comforting or frustrating to you that the psalmists' emotions are recorded in Scripture?

9. What is your favorite thing you read about God's character in your God Shots from this week?

DAYS 127–133

1. What can we learn from the fact that even David's good desire gets a no from God?

2. How does God's response supersede David's request?

3. Psalm 25 tells us that God instructs the humble. Why is humility a necessary trait for a learner to possess? How can a person learn humility if they don't possess it?

4. Think of all the ways the story of David and Mephibosheth mirrors our story with Christ. What does Mephibosheth have to offer David? What does David have to offer Mephibosheth? Who seeks out whom? What other things come to mind here that point us to the story of God and His people?

5. Read Psalm 75:1 aloud. One by one, recount one of God's wondrous deeds to you personally from the past week.

6. Read Psalm 20:4 aloud. We've all asked God for things that we're grateful He answered with a no. How does remembering those instances help us rightly view verses like this?

7. Some people believe those in the Old Testament were saved by works and sacrifices. But this week we saw a lot of Scripture pointing to God's plan to redeem people *through the work of Christ*. We saw it in Psalm 50 where God says sacrifices aren't sufficient; He's after their *hearts*. We saw it in Psalm 65:3, where David says *God* atones for his sins. How do these passages in the Old Testament show a through line of grace and the provision of Christ's death even for those who lived before He was born on earth as a human?

8. Despite God's unique covenant with the nation-state of Israel, He's already showing us that He has plans to save people from among every nation, and He's planting that desire in the hearts of His people. Read Psalm 67 aloud. What nations or people has God given you a heart to see Him save? Who do you hope comes to know and praise Him?

9. Was it hard to see David sin on so many levels? Why do we often want to make heroes out of humans in Scripture? Why is it important for us not to do that?

10. What is your favorite thing you read about God's character in your God Shots from this week?

1. In Psalm 32, David expresses the weight of carrying around his unconfessed sins and walking in unrepentance. Even though God put away his sin and it was paid for by Jesus on the cross, he still finds freedom in confession and encourages others to confess their sins too. What formal or informal practices of reflection, confession, and repentance do you have in place in your life?

2. David's kingdom begins to fracture as his sons repeat his sin patterns. Their sins come as the consequences of his own, but they also mirror his own in a lot of ways. What are some ways we can respond righteously and wickedly to the consequences of our sins? How can experiencing the consequences of our sins serve as God's tool to sanctify us and point us toward righteousness?

3. As David prays for God to bless and sustain him, he also prays for God to thwart his enemies. What determines whether prayers like this are righteous and godly or arrogant and selfish? If David's enemies are praying the same prayers, how does God determine who gets a yes and who gets a no?

4. Read Psalm 40:1–3 aloud. What spiritual discipline is represented in this passage? Read Psalm 40:9–10 aloud. What different

spiritual discipline is represented in this passage? Which one of these spiritual disciplines do you struggle with the most?

5. David pardons Shimei, and he makes a peaceful resolution between Ziba and Mephibosheth even though Ziba deliberately lied to him. Are his actions simply a diplomatic move as a king who is trying to stabilize his kingdom? Or are they motivated by a pure heart? Try to discuss the situation through each possible lens.

6. What does God's response to Saul's sins reveal about the way He relates to Israel as a whole? Is this how He always acts? Or is this because of His unique covenant relationship with Israel?

7. Read Psalm 5:4–7 aloud. Which of the evil actions described pertain to David? Why does he have such confidence that he can draw near to God?

8. In Psalm 38, David has lots of troubles—physical, emotional, spiritual, relational—yet he asks for God's nearness above and beyond all other rescue. Why do you think that is his chief request?

9. What is your favorite thing you read about God's character in your God Shots from this week?

1. David makes some shocking claims about his righteousness in his song in 2 Samuel 22:21–25. What do you think he's trying to accomplish? Is he trying to keep up appearances in front of the people? Does he think God has forgotten? Or is he pointing to something else altogether?

2. Read Psalm 97:10 and Psalm 99:8 aloud. How do these two verses illustrate the same ideas? Do these ideas feel at odds to you, or do they feel like they complement each other?

3. Scripture tells us that both God and Satan incited David to take the census (2 Samuel 24:1 and 1 Chronicles 21:1). How could these two passages work together?

4. For the king to take a census when God commands it is obedience, but for the king to take a census when God doesn't command it is sinful. What are some areas of life where you want to take the liberty to "take your own census" after He has set up boundaries?

5. Assuming the Angel of the LORD *is* the preincarnate Jesus, is it challenging to think of Him fulfilling the Father's assignment in 1 Chronicles 21:14–16? Why or why not?

6. The Levites are assigned their roles in the temple *not* on the basis of their passions or giftings but based on their genealogies. For much of history this has been the case—for people to follow in the career path set by their ancestors; only in recent years have we become more individualized. It's easy for us to see how God can work in our individual stories since that's our cultural perspective, but how can you see God at work in the story of these family occupations? How are His character and plan revealed through that process?

7. Read Psalm 138:8 aloud. Where do you like to put the emphasis in this verse? Why is that particular emphasis most meaningful to you?

8. Read Psalm 139:16 aloud. Does it feel comforting or threatening to think of God having all your days written before you even existed? Why?

9. Solomon is the son of David and Bathsheba, whose relationship is marred by sin upon sin. What does it reveal about God that He chooses Solomon to be Israel's king and His temple-builder?

10. What is your favorite thing you read about God's character in your God Shots from this week?

1. Read Psalm 115:3 and Psalm 115:16 aloud. Does verse 16 mean God isn't active on earth? Or does it mean something different? How can these two verses work together?

2. Knowing David died with murder or revenge on his heart, but that Scripture includes him in the Hall of Faith, what does this reveal about God and His relationship with His kids? Do you find that frustrating, encouraging, or confusing? Why?

3. Read Psalm 37:4 aloud. What are some ways this verse could be interpreted apart from the commonly accepted view? What are some potential dangers of misunderstanding or misapplying this verse?

4. Read Psalm 119:71 and 119:75 aloud. Have you ever praised God for your afflictions? How has He used them to grow you, teach you, and bless you?

5. Which aspect of God's Word do you tend to rely on most—the "lamp" aspect for the specific guidance of your daily steps, or the "light" aspect for wider, general guidance? How can you lean into using God's Word more for the one you're less inclined toward?

6. Read 1 Kings 3:13 aloud, then read Deuteronomy 17:16–17 aloud. Why would God give Solomon something He has told kings not to accumulate? Does anything else in the context of 1 Kings 3 reveal why Solomon might be able to handle this gift well?

7. Do you view Song of Solomon more as a story about human love or as an allegory about God's love for His people? Why?

8. Read Proverbs 3:5–7 aloud. Can you think of a time when following God meant going against your desires or your natural instincts? Which path did you choose? In retrospect, how do you feel about that decision?

9. What is your favorite thing you read about God's character in your God Shots from this week?

1. Is it challenging to read the book of Proverbs through the lens of it being wisdom literature instead or promises or prophecies? Why or why not? And if so, how?

2. Read Proverbs 8:13 aloud. What kinds of evil are especially easy for you to hate? What kinds of evil are hard for you to hate? Why?

3. The book of Proverbs has a lot to say about what we say. It addresses those of us who speak up at the wrong times or in the wrong ways *and* those of us who don't speak up when we should. Which area do you struggle with most? Was there a particular verse that stood out to you this week that pertains to our words?

4. Proverbs praises the wise and encourages us to seek wise counsel and wise friends. Who is the wisest person you know? In what areas or ways do they demonstrate wisdom? What do you admire most about them?

5. Many of the proverbs talk about the wisdom of being slow to anger and not being quarrelsome in general. What are some things worth being angry over and worth fighting against? How does Scripture point to the wisdom of those things? Can you think of a

time when Scripture records God demonstrating anger? What was God angry about?

6. Read Proverbs 24:3–4 aloud. Which of these do you want to see God increase in you the most: wisdom, understanding, or knowledge?

7. Throughout all of this week's chapters, Solomon listed several things that the wise avoid. Which is a struggle for you to avoid? Which can you thank God for helping you overcome?

8. What is your favorite thing you read about God's character in your God Shots from this week?

1. Has studying the temple and its significance impacted the way you view the phrase "my body is a temple"? What are some common misunderstandings about this phrase?

2. Read 1 Kings 8:41–43 aloud. In the ancient Near East, each nation has their own god or gods. In their view, crossing a border means crossing into the territory of a different god's reign. Knowing that, why do you think Solomon prays for other nations to know YHWH?

3. God's presence is so intense that people can't touch or directly look at the ark of the covenant, and so thick in the temple that the priests fall down to worship. Despite all that, they *want* to be near God and go to great lengths to build a temple for Him to dwell in. Have you ever felt God's presence at work in you in a powerful way?

4. Why is it important to remember who God is speaking to when He makes promises like the one in 2 Chronicles 7:14? What can go wrong when we misapply God's promises?

5. Instead of aiming to apply a promise for ourselves that isn't specifically for us, we can aim to learn something about God and His

character from those verses. What can we learn about God's character from 2 Chronicles 7:14?

6. Read Psalm 150:2 aloud. This verse praises God for His "mighty deeds" and His "excellent greatness." The first focuses on what He does, and the second focuses on who He is. How are those two things different, and why is that important?

7. Not all pagans hate or oppose Solomon. His wisdom and ambition earn him the favor of foreign rulers who oppose YHWH (like King Hiram of Tyre and the queen of Sheba), but his desire to keep peace leads him to cross the line of wisdom and righteousness through his marriage alliance with the pagan daughter of the Egyptian pharaoh. What's one area of your life where people-pleasing or peacekeeping tempts you to cross a boundary into unrighteousness?

8. When Solomon gives wisdom that seems to be contradictory (Proverbs 26:4–5), what is he revealing about life and wisdom?

9. What is your favorite thing you read about God's character in your God Shots from this week?

1. Read Proverbs 28:5 aloud. This verse frees us from trying to be understood by those who don't love God. What's something you thought was foolish before you started following Jesus but now see as wise and good?

2. Read Ecclesiastes 4:4 aloud. Do you agree with the preacher's summary here? Why or why not? How have you seen the vanity of comparison stealing your focus from the eternal things God has called us to focus on?

3. What did you think of the preacher's experiment in Ecclesiastes? Did any of his conclusions surprise you?

4. Despite having all the blessings of wealth and power, Solomon still makes sacrifices to gods besides YHWH. These pagan sacrifices are generally offered in hopes of getting *more*. Have you ever seen syncretism creep into your own life? What other "sources of spiritual power" (astrology, psychics, mantras, manifestation, etc.) have you been tempted to look to for help?

5. Has your view of Proverbs 31 changed at all over the course of our study? If so, how?

6. After King Rehoboam's older, trusted advisors tell him to be kind to his servants, he goes to his friends to ask for their advice, and they tell him to dial up his oppressive rule. What does it reveal about King Rehoboam that he seeks and follows the counsel of his friends instead?

7. Read 1 Kings 12:15 aloud. What role is God playing in what happens with King Rehoboam and his advisors? Why?

8. King Jeroboam's fears lead him to control and idolatry as he tries to duplicate God's temple in the northern kingdom. What would have been an appropriate response to his scenario and fear?

9. Based on what you've seen from both kingdoms so far—the Northern Kingdom of Israel with King Jeroboam and the Southern Kingdom of Judah with King Rehoboam—which kingdom would you prefer to live in and why? In this division, which kingdom do you think God will show more favor and mercy?

10. What is your favorite thing you read about God's character in your God Shots from this week?

DAYS 176–182

1. In his early years, King Asa makes massive reforms for God's glory. But in his final years, he resists rebukes and consequences and he tortures a prophet of God and some of his people. What do you think prompts this shift in Asa's heart?

2. Read 2 Chronicles 17:6 aloud. The second half of the verse reveals one of the ways Jehoshaphat demonstrates the first half of the verse. Look around the room and consider this: What are some ways others in this group have demonstrated courage in the ways of the Lord? How have you seen them honor God in the midst of worldliness and idolatry?

3. Elijah sees God's mighty displays of power but also has small moments of closeness with Him. In your own life, what has impacted your relationship with God most—big miraculous acts or private moments of conversation? Why?

4. For most of his life, King Ahab seems interested in receiving only the favorable words of the prophets, not the warnings or rebukes. Does that resonate with you on any level? If so, how?

   (Follow-up: The encouraging news for all of us is that God draws us to repentance, just like He did with Ahab! The fact that you're here today is evidence that God hasn't given up on you!)

5. Despite King Ahab's wickedness, God is repeatedly merciful and gracious to him. He grants him victory twice over King Ben-hadad of Syria, and He relaxes his punishment by delaying it until the next generation. What does this reveal about God and His character?

6. When King Jehoshaphat leads his people out to war against the coalition, he says, "Believe in the LORD your God, and you will be established; believe his prophets, and you will succeed" (2 Chronicles 20:20). They believed and won the battle, but 20:33 says, "The people had not yet set their hearts upon the God of their fathers." How is "believing in God" different from "setting your heart on Him"?

7. Even though Israel's distress is the result of their sin, God judges Edom for not helping them. Read Obadiah 1:12–14 aloud. This is God's instruction to Edom about how to treat Israel. What do we learn about God's character from the way He cares for His kids when they sin?

8. Read Psalm 82:1 aloud. Based on what we've learned so far, how does this verse correspond to Scripture's teaching on monotheism?

9. What is your favorite thing you read about God's character in your God Shots from this week?

1. What do you think Elisha means when he asks for a double portion of Elijah's spirit?

2. Do you believe Elijah dies in 2 Kings 1 or that he is just carried away? What Scriptures led you to that conclusion?

3. Naaman, the Syrian military commander, is angry at God's appointed means of healing. What's something God has healed in you through a process that frustrated you? How did you respond to God in the moment? And how have you responded to God in retrospect?

4. It may be hard for some to accept the idea of Jehu killing all of Ahab's descendants and the prophets of Baal. When we bump into these things, it's helpful to zoom out and recall that they've all earned the death penalty through their sins. They also participate in human sacrifice, bestiality, and summoning demons, among other evil rituals. Does remembering that help clarify more about God's intentions behind His commands to Jehu? Why or why not?

5. When Israel experiences God's judgment in the form of a Syrian attack, King Jehoahaz seeks God—but only for the sake of relief, not because he actually wants to repent. How can you discern

what your motives are when you're seeking God? What can you do if your motives are impure or selfish?

6. Despite the fact that Northern Israel shows no real signs of repentance and continues in their sins and idolatry, God spares them. Why? What does this reveal about God and His character?

7. Jonah doesn't want God to show mercy to the Ninevites. What does it reveal about our hearts if or when there are people we hope God doesn't adopt into His family? What does it reveal about God's heart that He can and does pursue His enemies?

8. This week we encountered King Amaziah, also called Uzziah, another king who starts off with humility, then grows strong in power, then becomes arrogant. Why is this cycle so easy to fall into? What actions or heart attitudes are necessary to remain humble and avoid becoming arrogant?

9. What is your favorite thing you read about God's character in your God Shots from this week?

1. If you were the people of Judah and you heard Isaiah's prophecy about how God hates your offerings and sacrifice, what would you think? How would you respond to this rebuke?

2. In Isaiah 6, God tells Isaiah to speak a rebuke to a people who won't listen. Why would God do this?

3. Read Amos 3:2 aloud. Is it troubling, surprising, or expected that God treats His kids differently from how He treats those who don't know Him? Why?

4. In all the woes and rebukes of the book of Amos, what themes did you notice? What seems to be especially heavy on God's heart during this time? What does that reveal to you about God's heart?

5. Read Isaiah 12:1–2 aloud. Do you feel and believe this? If so, what's one way you've seen God's strength show up in your life? What "song" has He given you to sing?

6. As we continue to read through more major and minor prophets, what pattern do you see emerging between the prophets' warnings, the people's responses, and God's actions?

7. During the reign of King Ahaz of Judah, he has a priest build a pagan altar, and the priests who are called to Samaria to teach the pagans how to live are mingling their worship with pagan worship. We expect more of the priests, but considering how priests are appointed for the job, why is this less of a surprise?

8. What is your favorite thing you read about God's character in your God Shots from this week?

1. Starting in chapter 13, Isaiah addresses the nations that are Israel's enemies. Some get the punishment they deserve, but to others, God shows mercy and doesn't give them what they deserve. What does this reveal about God's heart? Is this frustrating or comforting to you? Why?

2. God's enemies, like the nation of Babylon, have hearts that rage against Him and His people. God turns their wickedness back on them, using it as a tool in His hands to lead His people to repent. According to your current understanding, is this unfair, beautiful, confusing, or something else? Why?

3. Isaiah prophesies against Jerusalem in chapter 22, and he says they'll ignore the obvious and lean into lives of excess instead. Do you tend to face hard times directly or avoid them? What lies, truths, fears, and/or desires prompt that response? Can you think of a response that would be more honoring to God? How would it feel to respond that way instead?

4. Read Isaiah 26:3 aloud. Both practically and spiritually, how can you aim to *know* God, *trust* God, and *fix your mind on* God?

5. Psalm 48 says to tell the next generation about God. Who is the first person who talked to you about God *rightly*? What about that conversation made Him seem interesting or beautiful to you?

6. According to Hosea 4:6, the downfall of the people of Israel is their "lack of knowledge" of God. Do you think this points more to a head knowledge, a heart knowledge, or both? How are the two connected? How have we seen Israel demonstrate this lack of knowledge?

7. In your own life, how have you benefited from an *increased* knowledge of God as we've moved through this study? How have you seen it change your heart and your mind?

8. In Hosea's prophecy, the people have turned away from God because of their abundance. How might abundance contribute to a lack of knowledge of God? Are you drawn more to God in times of abundance and ease or times of lack and trial?

9. In many of Isaiah's "woes," he points out that the people live in autonomy instead of surrender to God. For you, what is the hardest part about not being autonomous in your everyday life?

10. What is your favorite thing you read about God's character in your God Shots from this week?

1. In Isaiah's six woes, he warns against relying on autonomy for our guidance and on others for our strength, particularly those who are God's enemies. However, there have been times when God has chosen to use His enemies to help His people or speak wisdom to them. How can we tell if it's a time when we need to lean into the wisdom or help of God's enemies versus a time when we should avoid them?

2. Read the following verses aloud: Proverbs 26:4–5 and Matthew 7:6 and 10:14. When the Assyrians taunt the people of Judah and wrongly misunderstand their faith in YHWH, the people remain silent in accordance with King Hezekiah's command. How can we know if the best response in a given situation is to correct someone and defend the truth (i.e., answer a fool) *or* to keep silent (i.e., don't answer a fool, keep your pearls, shake the dust off your sandals)?

3. In Isaiah 38:17, King Hezekiah says, "Behold, it was for my welfare that I had great bitterness," but then he ends the thought by saying, *"But in love you have delivered my life from the pit of destruction."* If you've ever felt bitterness toward God, was it based on an area where you felt He was holding out on you? If so, what has God done over time to reveal more of His heart to bless you?

4. Isaiah 42:1–4 is a prophecy of Jesus. Read it aloud and look for the aspects of God's character that are revealed. Which part is most surprising, encouraging, or comforting to you? Since Jesus is the exact imprint of the Father's nature (Hebrews 1:3), can you think of times when the Father has displayed these same traits?

5. Babylon has set their hearts to do evil at every turn. Isaiah says God will use their evil intentions as a tool to bring Israel, His people, to repentance, and then He will punish Babylon for it. Is it unjust for God to punish Babylon for this? Why or why not?

6. Many of the psalms we read this week referenced specific incidents from Israel's history in their relationship with YHWH. As we read these psalms, how can we connect with the truth of them on a personal and spiritual level if they were written about someone else's experience?

7. Isaiah 53:10 speaks of Jesus's crucifixion and says, "It was the will of the LORD to crush him." According to Revelation 13:8, this has always been the plan, and John 18:4 says Jesus knew all He would endure, yet He willingly submitted to the plan to be crushed on our behalf. How does it impact your view of the Father to know that He has never planned to punish you for your sins?

8. How does it impact your view of Jesus to know that He willingly took on your punishment?

9. What is your favorite thing you read about God's character in your God Shots from this week?

1. Isaiah 57:18 says, "I have seen his ways, but I will heal him." Where do you go when you sin? Do you run to God, knowing His love, comfort, and healing wait for you there? Or do you run from God, afraid He's disappointed in you?

2. Prior to Israel being led into captivity as a consequence of breaking the covenant, God warns them repeatedly to repent, but He says they won't. Then He keeps reminding them that their exile will be temporary and that He will restore more than they've lost. Why do you think it's important to Him to keep reiterating the blessing that awaits them on the other side of exile instead of just the warning to repent?

3. As the book of Isaiah closes, God paints a picture of His eternal kingdom and reiterates that people from every language and nation will be included. Why is it significant and helpful for us to see these promises written by the Old Testament prophets, and not just in the New Testament?

4. King Hezekiah's heart is distracted from God by his abundance. Abundance of any kind—whether it's financial, relational, medicinal, or vocational—can distance our hearts from God. None of those things are necessarily bad on their own, but they become idols when they displace God. Have you seen that happen in your own life? How did you get free from that place?

5. Hezekiah and his son Manasseh live opposite lives. Hezekiah starts humble and near to God and dies proud. Manasseh starts proud and far from God and dies faithful. What is the turning point for each of them? What can we learn from their experiences?

6. Read Nahum 1:2–3 aloud. Read Exodus 34:6–7 aloud. Is it hypocritical of God to treat His kids differently from how He treats His enemies? Why or why not?

7. In Josiah's days, the people of God have lost the Word of God in the house of God, and their lives reflect it. The very people who are called by God's name don't even realize it's missing until it's found. In what ways do you think the people of God are missing His Word today? Imagine the positive changes that would occur if we took Him and His Word seriously and prioritized it in our lives! What changes has God brought to your own life as you've begun to cherish His Word?

8. The Egyptian pharaoh Neco appoints one of Judah's final kings, Jehoiakim. Thinking back to the early kings of Israel, who used to appoint them? What does this transition represent in the timeline of Israel's relationship with YHWH?

9. What is your favorite thing you read about God's character in your God Shots from this week?

1. Read Zephaniah 3:9–10 aloud. Given the context, what do you think God means when He says, "I will change the speech of the peoples to a pure speech"?

2. As we continue reading through the major and minor prophets, we're learning a lot about their lives. As an overarching theme, how are their roles and lives different from what you may have heard or expected? Which prophets, or which of their stories, have surprised you most?

3. The prophets repeatedly describe an "undoing" of creation, where the earth will be emptied out, then follow it with prophecies of the world flourishing again. What do you think when you read these prophecies? Is it scary, exciting, confusing? Is it odd to imagine living on *earth* in the eternal kingdom? (See Isaiah 65:17 and Revelation 21:2.)

4. Read Jeremiah 9:23–24 aloud. Think about the things you're tempted to boast in. Think about what's underneath your desire to boast in those things and be identified in that way. What would it look like for you to be known and identified *more* by your affiliation with the God of the universe instead? How would it change your approach to life if you were primarily concerned

with displaying *His* characteristics—steadfast love, justice, and righteousness?

5. Jeremiah 12:2 says, "You are near in their mouth and far from their heart." Has this ever been true for you? Did you realize it at the time? What was the catalyst for change?

6. The prophets repeatedly speak about the fact that God is going to welcome outsiders into His family—people who aren't Israelites. How do you think the Israelites felt when they kept hearing this news from prophet after prophet after prophet? How would you have felt?

7. Read Jeremiah 17:5–6 aloud. How would you describe this man? What is he like to be around?

8. Read Jeremiah 17:7–8 aloud. How would you describe this man? What is he like to be around?

9. Read Genesis 2:7, Isaiah 45:9, and Jeremiah 18:5–6 aloud. What is encouraging about these verses and their theme? What is challenging about these verses and their theme?

10. What is your favorite thing you read about God's character in your God Shots from this week?

1. Imagine you are in the crowd when Jeremiah has his showdown with Hananiah, the false prophet. Jeremiah is wearing a yoke and saying you'll need to submit to the yoke of Babylon's king. Hananiah is saying God has broken the yoke and will bring all the people and the blessings back home within two years. Which prophet would you believe? Would your belief be purely based on desires and emotions? Or would you be prompted to examine yourself and to recall what you know of God's Word?

2. Read Jeremiah 29:10–14 aloud. We love to recall verse 11 as comfort, but what are these people about to endure as a part of God's plan for their lives? What will it ultimately produce in them? Overall, what seems to be the primary thing Jeremiah is aiming to convey in this section?

3. Jeremiah has commanded the people to invest in the place of their exile while they're there for seventy years, but then God will bring them back to the promised land. Why would they be tempted to stay behind in Babylon? What would it reveal about their hearts if they stayed behind? What spiritual dangers might that lead them into?

4. Jeremiah references a future Jerusalem, saying, "[It] shall be sacred to the LORD. It shall not be uprooted or overthrown anymore forever" (31:40). Read Revelation 3:12 and 21:1–2 aloud. According to your current understanding, what is the relationship between the old heaven and earth, the new heaven and earth, and the new Jerusalem? What will happen to the place we currently call heaven?

5. Read Jeremiah 32:40 aloud. What part of this verse is most comforting to you? Is any part of it difficult for you? Why?

6. The story of the Rechabites (Jeremiah 35) reveals a lot about both them and the Israelites, but what does it reveal about God?

7. God loves to use outsiders to rescue His people and then bless them as a result. From Rahab in the book of Joshua to Ebed-melech in the book of Jeremiah. And in the New Testament, Jesus tells a parable about a Samaritan who offers help to a wounded traveler (who is presumably Jewish). With Rahab and Ebed-melech, He also invites them into His family! What does it reveal about God that He doesn't just exalt the Israelites but that He paints outsiders in a positive light and gives them important roles?

8. How did it feel to see the people of Judah carted off into exile—out of Jerusalem, the city it took them so long to conquer in the land it took them so long to get to? According to 2 Chronicles 36:21, what is God granting the land?

9. What is your favorite thing you read about God's character in your God Shots from this week?

1. Which of the five "woes" of Babylon is most tempting for you to put your hope in—wealth, security, power, pleasure, or control? What emotions or desires are connected to that specific area that make it such an alluring thing to aim for?

2. Why do you think the people of Judah don't believe Jeremiah and his prophecies, even after Jerusalem falls like he prophesied?

3. It's easy to focus on God's destruction and think of Him harshly in the final chapters of Jeremiah. But what unexpected mercies does He show toward both His enemies and His people? What does that reveal about His character?

4. Read Jeremiah 50:34 aloud. What aspects of God's character and His plan are revealed in this verse? How would you summarize it?

5. What was most troubling to you in the book of Jeremiah's prophecies and their fulfillment? Why?

6. What was most encouraging or eye-opening to you in the book of Jeremiah? Why?

7. The book of Lamentations attributes Jerusalem's destruction to God, even though their sin was the cause and He repeatedly warned them it would happen if they didn't repent. Do you find God's actions hard to accept? Why or why not?

8. Even though Lamentations is filled with accusations against God, the author ends with praise and a request for God to draw near. What does the author seem to understand about God after all he's been through? What helps a person develop that kind of response and insight?

9. What is your favorite thing you read about God's character in your God Shots from this week?

DAYS 239–245

1. In Ezekiel 1, what is the significance of God showing up in all His glory in Babylon?

2. Why do you think God puts such an emphasis on both His people and His enemies knowing that He is the LORD?

3. What things in your life (circumstances, experiences, people, etc.) have helped you come to believe that He is the LORD?

4. What are some of the ways the Israelites have struggled to adjust to a spiritual mind-set instead of a *cultural* mind-set? In what ways do you struggle to do the same?

5. Read Ezekiel 11:19–20 aloud. What are the implications of what God is promising in these verses? In what ways is this different from the relationship God has had with Israel up to this point? When does or did this change occur?

6. In Ezekiel 14:1–8, the rebellious elders come to seek God's counsel. He agrees to speak with them but says He won't answer their requests for guidance; He'll only address their idolatry. Why is this

the best and wisest type of response? Have you ever had a similar experience in your relationship with God?

7. Read Ezekiel 17:23–24 aloud. What do you think God is communicating to the Israelites through this metaphor and prophecy?

8. Read Ezekiel 18:23 and 18:32 aloud. If these verses are true, how do we explain all the passages where God commands or causes death?

9. God finds no righteous people among Israel. He calls them all "dross." Based on your current understanding and what you've seen in the story of their relationship, do you agree with God's assessment?

10. Given that the people of Israel are consistently rebellious, why does God continue to speak to them about restoration?

11. What is your favorite thing you read about God's character in your God Shots from this week?

DAYS 246–252

1. In his role as a prophet, Ezekiel often has to experience various kinds of personal pain that will give him credibility when addressing the people. What important characteristics would this help develop in a prophet? What does it reveal to us about God that He wants His prophets to develop those characteristics?

2. Based on your current understanding, what do you think happened with Ezekiel's prophecy about Tyre in Ezekiel 27–28? Was it fulfilled and merely infused with metaphor? Did Tyre repent and avoid total disaster? Did it merely happen on a different timeline than the other prophecies?

3. Read Ezekiel 28:11–19 aloud. What conclusion did you reach about whom this prophecy (which is given to Tyre) refers to?

4. Read Ezekiel 33:13 aloud. How does this verse dispel the idea that God weighs our good and bad deeds on a scale to determine our eternal destinies?

5. Read Ezekiel 35:4 aloud, then read 36:9–11 aloud. In both passages, God is taking action to make Himself known to people, but the actions are completely different. Consider the context. What

accounts for such different actions? What does this reveal about God and His character, plan, and motives?

6. In the vision of the dry bones in Ezekiel 37, God doesn't command the bodies to breathe; instead, He commands the breath to enter the bodies. Do you think there is any spiritual significance to this? If so, what is it?

7. In chapter 42, Ezekiel's temple vision records that the wall is "to make a separation between the holy and the common." What might be some wrong ways to interpret the meaning and implications of this passage? What might be some right ways to interpret its meaning and implications?

8. What is your favorite thing you read about God's character in your God Shots from this week?

DAYS 253–259

1. In every day's reading up until the final three days of Ezekiel, where he shares his temple vision, God repeatedly uses the phrase "they shall know that I am the Lord." By some counts, it shows up roughly seventy times. Do you think there's any significance in that number?

2. Why do you think God stops using that phrase when He starts describing the temple?

3. In all the dimensions and descriptions in Ezekiel's temple vision, what stood out to you most? Why?

4. Read Joel 2:27 and 3:17 aloud. This book was likely written around the same time as the book of Ezekiel, and it references the same phrase that God spoke through Ezekiel repeatedly. Why do you think both prophets referenced the same phrase?

5. King Nebuchadnezzar quickly goes from giving praise to YHWH for Daniel's dream interpretation skills to building a statue in honor of himself. Can you think of a time when your heart pivoted quickly from God to self or something else?

6. In Daniel 4, God speaks to Nebuchadnezzar through dreams, through Daniel, and through an audible voice. Which form of communication might be easiest to misunderstand or misinterpret? What might be helpful in knowing this communication is all from God?

7. Do you believe God has spoken to you through a dream? If so, what was that experience like and how did you respond to it?

8. When you read the prophetic books of Scripture, what is your intellectual and/or emotional response? Do you find it hard to look for God and His character instead of just looking for a forecast of the future? What do our responses reveal about our hearts?

9. What did you learn from or appreciate most about Daniel's sneak peek into the spiritual realm in chapters 10–12?

10. What is your favorite thing you read about God's character in your God Shots from this week?

1. Read Ezra 1:2–3 aloud and listen for what Cyrus believes about God and himself. Where does Cyrus claim dominion? Who gave him that dominion? Where does Cyrus claim God is located? What insights does all this information give us into what Cyrus believes about God and himself?

2. In Ezra 5, the prophets Haggai and Zechariah speak to the returned exiles in Jerusalem, and their encouragement prompts them to begin rebuilding the temple. Why do you think the people are willing to listen to and respond to these prophets but wouldn't listen to or respond to the prophets who called them to repent before the exile?

3. Read Haggai 1:9 aloud. Why is God thwarting their plans? When you encounter thwarted plans, who do you naturally tend to blame—God, Satan, yourself, someone else? How can we determine whether we're supposed to keep trying, change course, or stop altogether?

4. Read Zechariah 2:8–11 aloud. In this passage, God references or addresses the other nations who oppose Israel (vv. 8–9), Israel (v. 10), and the other nations again (v. 11). In the two references to the other nations, there's a vast difference in the way God says He

will treat them. What accounts for this difference? What does this reveal about God, His character, and/or His plan?

5. Read Zechariah 5:3–4 aloud. Then read 8:16–17 aloud. What connections do you notice between the vision of the flying scroll and God's commands to the people? Why do you think God emphasizes these things? What does this reveal about what God values?

6. In the final chapter of Zechariah, he recounts a vision of the coming day of the LORD, including descriptions of Jerusalem and its architecture and landscapes, but makes no mention of the temple. If the temple has been such a focus of Jerusalem, why is there no mention of it in this vision of the future?

7. Based on your current understanding, do you think a third temple will be built? Why or why not?

8. Despite the fact that God's name never appears in the book of Esther, He's evident behind the scenes throughout the story. Where did you notice His stealth activity most?

9. What is your favorite thing you read about God's character in your God Shots from this week?

1. Scripture describes Ezra as being "skilled in the law of Moses" (7:6). His knowledge of the Word gives him an increased understanding of God's sovereignty. In fact, he credits God with a wide variety of things: the kindness of the pagan king of Persia (7:27), the provision of staff (8:18), protection on their journey (8:31), and favor in the midst of their slavery (9:8). How have you seen your view of God increase as you've studied the Word?

2. Both Ezra and Nehemiah have confessed the sins of the people, not just their own personal sins. While we're only held accountable for our own sins in the scheme of eternity, Scripture seems to demonstrate a measure of responsibility for how we resolve corporate sins on earth. Read the following verses aloud and discuss how you've seen them applied in Ezra and Nehemiah specifically. Corporate sin and responsibility: Exodus 20:5, Jeremiah 32:18, Lamentations 5:7. Individual sin and responsibility: Deuteronomy 24:16, Ezekiel 18:20.

3. How would you describe the prayer in Nehemiah 9:6–38? The only request it makes of God is for Him to take notice of their current state of affliction (v. 32). How is this kind of prayer fitting for a corporate setting? Why would a different kind of prayer be more suited to a private setting?

4. In the Hebrew Old Testament, Ezra and Nehemiah are one book of history (not two); their timeline and location often overlap. What similarities and contrasts do you see between the two leaders? Which leader are you drawn to most? Why?

5. Malachi points out strong contrasts between Jacob and Esau. If you had a chance to research this, what do you think he was pointing to? Here are some popular options: (a) God hated Esau the person; (b) by comparison, God loved Esau less than Jacob; (c) this refers to the two people groups, not necessarily the individual people; (d) this text reveals that God isn't bound by the cultural norms to show preference to the firstborn. What is hardest about this passage for you? Why?

6. If God were to love one sinner but hate another, which person would get what they deserved from God? Which person would get what they didn't deserve? How does this help us as we wrestle with the Jacob/Esau question above?

7. The end of the book of Malachi describes two fires—the oven to burn up the evildoers and the sun of righteousness that brings healing. How might this idea of fire serving two opposite purposes for two different types of people connect with the Jacob/Esau question from the beginning of the book?

8. How do these two fires disprove the people's two accusations of God in 2:17?

9. What is your favorite thing you read about God's character in your God Shots from this week?

1. The first humans to confirm or acknowledge that Mary is pregnant with the Messiah are the unborn John the Baptist and the elderly Elizabeth. What does it reveal about God that these are His two choices for the first prophecies (physical and audible) about Jesus's identity?

2. Read Luke 2:29–32 aloud. What do you think Simeon means by his words in verse 32? Why is this important to note?

3. What new things did you notice or learn about the birth of Christ?

4. Through Simeon's prophecy about Jesus being a light to all the nations (Luke 2:32) and the wise men coming to worship Jesus from far away in the east, we're starting to see that the Jewish Messiah is actually going to rescue more people than the Jews. How do you think this message will go over with the Jews?

5. Read Matthew 3:9 aloud. What is the heart of the message that John the Baptist is communicating here? Why is this important?

6. We see the three persons of the Trinity serving in distinct roles at Jesus's baptism. Can you think of other places in Scripture where

we see them working together simultaneously or where they reference or point to each other? How does this help us understand their roles and functions?

7. Which of the three persons of the Trinity (Father, Son, Spirit) are you most inclined toward and why? Which is the most challenging for you to connect with?

8. Read John 10:30, John 14:26, Colossians 1:15, and Hebrews 1:3 aloud. What do these verses reveal about unity of the Trinity? Does this help resolve any connections that are challenging for you? Why or why not?

9. What buttons does Jesus seem to already be pushing with His messages? Is this surprising? Why or why not?

10. Why do you think Jesus is reserved with some miracles and more demonstrative with others?

11. What is your favorite thing you read about God's character in your God Shots from this week?

1. The Pharisees repeatedly accuse Jesus of breaking the law. On a spiritual level, why is this impossible?

2. In what ways do we sometimes act like Pharisees and "build a fence around the law"? What are some positive and negative things that can result from setting up our own standards? What are we trying to accomplish by putting our own standards in place?

3. How has this week's reading shaped or expanded your understanding of the Sabbath?

4. Read Matthew 12:30–37 aloud. Based on the context of this conversation and what you learned in this week's reading, can a Christian commit the sin of "blasphemy against the Spirit" (12:31)? Why or why not?

5. How has this week's reading shaped or expanded your understanding of Jesus's miraculous healings?

6. Read Matthew 11:25–26 aloud. What is Jesus praising the Father for in this passage?

7. Does it matter which person of the Trinity we address when we pray? Is it okay to just use the name God instead of being more specific? Why or why not?

8. Jesus has harsh words for the Pharisee and the lawyer in Luke 11:37–53. How does His response shape your view of Him? How does it shape your understanding of His purposes and goals in His conversations?

9. Consider Matthew 13 and the parable of the sower. At first Jesus is talking to a crowd that includes both people who are His disciples and followers and people who aren't. Later He talks only with His disciples. How do the members of Jesus's audiences impact what He shares? Where else have we seen Him adapt His message to be specific to the person or location?

10. What is your favorite thing you read about God's character in your God Shots from this week?

1. Read Mark 4:10–12 aloud. What do you think Jesus means by this? How does this quote from the prophet Isaiah connect with His answer here?

2. Read Mark 4:37–39 aloud. What does it reveal about Jesus that He doesn't rebuke the disciples for their fear in the storm but instead rebukes the storm itself?

3. In Matthew 10:22, Jesus is talking about the persecution the disciples will endure when they go out to preach the kingdom of God. He says, "The one who endures to the end will be saved." What does He mean by this?

4. Read Mark 6:51–52 aloud. What keeps the disciples from understanding Jesus? What does this reveal about head knowledge versus heart knowledge? What else can we learn from this passage?

5. Read John 6:28 aloud. What would you have expected Jesus to say in response to this question?

6. Read John 6:37 and 6:44 aloud. Reflecting on your own life, what were some of the tools God used to draw you to Himself?

7. When Jesus multiplies the loaves and fish the first time, there are twelve baskets left over. When He multiplies the loaves and fish the second time, there are seven baskets left over. What do you think these numbers symbolize? How has Jesus tailored this symbolism to each audience?

8. Read Matthew 16:24 aloud. What are the three steps of obedience Jesus addresses here? Which is the most challenging for you? Why?

9. Jesus warns His disciples against letting the teachings of the Pharisees creep into their beliefs. Based on what you know so far, how would you summarize the teachings of the Pharisees? How can we spot similar ideas when we encounter them in the world today?

10. Read Mark 9:30–32 aloud. Jesus explains His death clearly to the disciples. Why do you think they can't understand what He is saying will happen to Him?

11. What is your favorite thing you read about God's character in your God Shots from this week?

1. In Scripture, the heart is the seat of the will and emotions, so what is Jesus pointing to when He says forgiveness must come "from your heart"? What are some signs that you've forgiven someone from your heart? What are some signs that you've only offered forgiveness as a verbal acknowledgment?

2. Read John 7:24 aloud. What do you think Jesus means by this? How do we judge "with right judgment"? Does this contradict what He said in Matthew 7:1–3? Why or why not?

3. Jesus spends a lot of time in John 8:38–47 marking out the difference between God's kids and the sons of the devil. What stood out to you most in this passage? What ideas were challenging or new to you?

4. Read John 9:1–3 aloud. Do you tend to ask "why" questions like the disciples? If so, how was Jesus's response to their question challenging? How might His answer also be encouraging?

5. Reflect on the parable of the good Samaritan. Imagine you're the person in the ditch and Jesus is the one who came to your rescue. Who has He put in your life as the innkeeper? Who has He used to bring you healing and rest?

6. Read Luke 13:24–30 aloud. What are the main points Jesus seems to be making here? What parts are hard to process? Do you think He intends for these words to be challenging to His audience at the time? Do you think He intends for them to be challenging to us? Why or why not?

7. In Luke 15, Jesus has an audience that consists of groups that tend to be at odds with each other—sinners, tax collectors, and Pharisees. The first two are drawn to Jesus's message, and the latter are repulsed by it. When He tells three parables with the same primary theme, what messages do you think He is trying to communicate to each group?

8. Read Luke 17:3–4 aloud. According to this verse, what precedes forgiveness? Can you think of a place in Scripture where we're commanded to forgive those who are expressly unrepentant? How does God respond to the unrepentant?

9. Read Luke 17:20–21 aloud. How has this passage been misused in society today? What are the dangers of misunderstanding or misapplying Jesus's words here?

10. What is your favorite thing you read about God's character in your God Shots from this week?

1. According to John 11:54, raising Lazarus from the dead is a turning point for Jesus. How do the location and audience contribute to this turning point? What is He being mindful of by making this adjustment?

2. Read Luke 18:22 aloud. How does Jesus respond to the rich ruler? How is this different from the way He responds to the Pharisees? What do you think accounts for the difference in His response?

3. Read Matthew 19:10–12 aloud. What are the three types of eunuchs Jesus describes? Given the context, what do you think He means by the last type?

4. In Matthew 21:43, Jesus is speaking to the scribes and Pharisees, both of whom are leaders among the Jewish religious community in Jerusalem. They hold high standards and often accuse Jesus of breaking their laws, yet Jesus accuses *them* of not producing the fruit of God's kingdom. What does the fruit of God's kingdom look like if not strict obedience?

5. Which story impacted you more—the rich ruler turning *away* from Jesus or Zaccheus turning *to* Jesus? Why?

6. Read John 12:27–30 aloud. What words characterize Jesus's tone during this exchange? What does it reveal about Jesus that He shares this struggle openly? How can it serve as an encouragement and a model for you when you face trials?

7. Read Mark 11:23–24 aloud. What other verses on prayer help us expand our understanding of these passages? What's the danger in taking these verses out of the context of Scripture and isolating them? What might motivate a person to do that, as opposed to seeking a fuller understanding of Scripture's teaching on prayer?

8. When Jesus is asked about paying taxes to Caesar and the oppressive Roman regime, he affirms it should be done. Yet we also see Him demonstrate that same humility while putting His foot down with Herod and Pilate elsewhere in the Gospels. On a practical level, what does it look like to follow in His footsteps and humbly honor God by keeping the law while also rebelling against wicked authorities? How do we strike that balance of humility in both submission *and* action? Are there any areas where you personally struggle to find the balance? (Note: This is about places where you have a question about your own actions, *not* ways you think *others* miss the mark.)

9. What is your favorite thing you read about God's character in your God Shots from this week?

1. Read Matthew 23:3 aloud. What direction does Jesus give His followers about the actions of the scribes and Pharisees? Is this shocking? Why or why not?

2. Heeding Jesus's directions in Matthew 23:3 has more to do with knowing our own motives, as opposed to knowing the motives of others. It requires us to have a certain level of self-awareness or discernment. How can we grow in these areas? Have you ever been made aware of a blind spot in your life? How did that happen?

3. In Mark 13, Jesus talks with Peter, James, John, and Andrew and gives them information and instructions for what they will face. At the minimum, this text serves as *information* for us today, helping us understand what the early church endured and how Christ's prophecies were fulfilled. Do you think it also serves as *instruction* for us? Why or why not?

4. What are some ways we can practice "waiting well" as we wait for the return of Christ? What are some ways we can practice "staying awake" in the meantime?

5. Read Matthew 25:31–34, 41, and 46 aloud. What do these verses reveal about God and His character? What aspects of this are challenging for you?

6. All throughout Jesus's ministry we've seen Him working to maintain the timeline of His death. As the day approaches, He begins to reveal more information to His followers, despite the fact that He knows His betrayer is among them (John 6:70). In Matthew 26, He even reveals the means and day of His death. What do you think the group dynamic is like in the days leading up to His death? Imagine the scenario from the perspective of Jesus, His followers, and His betrayer.

7. Why do you think Jesus feeds the Lord's Supper to Judas? How do you think Judas feels about this?

8. Who is humbled in the act of foot washing? The one doing the washing, the one being washed, or both? Why?

9. What do you think of C.S. Lewis's statement that Jesus was either lunatic, liar, or Lord?* Is there another possible alternative? Why or why not?

10. What is your favorite thing you read about God's character in your God Shots from this week?

*C. S. Lewis, *Mere Christianity* (New York: HarperOne, 2001), 52.

1. Read Revelation 13:8 aloud. How many humans existed before the foundation of the world? If the cross has been the plan since before creation, what does that reveal about God and His character? What does it reveal about humanity?

2. Read Matthew 27:46 aloud. What do you think Jesus is communicating through this statement?

3. What new thing did you learn from the story of Jesus's crucifixion in this week's reading, or what stood out to you most? Why?

4. What new thing did you learn from the story of Jesus's resurrection in this week's reading, or what stood out to you most? Why?

5. How many fish do the apostles catch in the Sea of Galilee after the resurrection? Read Matthew 13:47 aloud. Do you think this verse from earlier in Jesus's ministry foreshadows this story? Why or why not? What are some of the implications of catching fish "of every kind"?

6. Based on your current understanding, how would you describe the event where the people in the early church were speaking other

languages in Acts 2? Why would this kind of sign be important for the early church?

7. Based on what happens with the Hellenist widows, what can we learn from the early church about how to handle the unique needs of a specific group within the church body? What's one modern problem this example from Acts 6 might help us resolve?

8. The apostles rejoice over being considered worthy to suffer for the sake of the gospel. Their prayers are focused around being able to speak the gospel *more*. What do you think gives them such a zeal for sharing the gospel and enduring pain, instead of seeking to protect themselves?

9. Persecution in Jerusalem launches the members of the early church out into the world to spread the gospel. God has a track record of using our trials for the good of His kingdom *and* for our joy! In what ways have you seen this be true in your own life?

10. What is your favorite thing you read about God's character in your God Shots from this week?

1. What is your favorite part of the story of Saul's conversion in Acts 9? Why? What does it reveal to you about God and His character?

2. Why is there so much complexity involved in spreading the gospel to the Gentiles? How does God work through both established and new members of the church to overcome the problem?

3. The circumcision party wants everyone to convert to Judaism before converting to Christianity. Is there anything in Scripture to support their point? What helps convince them they're wrong?

4. Read Acts 14:1–7 aloud. Under what circumstances are Paul and Barnabas willing to stay in Iconium? What changes that makes them decide to leave? Why do you think this is a turning point for them? What does this reveal about God and His plan for them in the spread of the gospel?

5. Why does Paul require circumcision for Timothy (Acts 16:1–5)? What lessons can we take from this that help us understand more about stumbling blocks? What lessons can we take from this that help us understand more about the requirements for leaders?

6. In Galatians (2:11–14), Paul mentions that he had to publicly rebuke Peter for failing to eat with the Gentiles and only eating with the Jews. What lessons can we take from this situation?

7. Read Galatians 4:6–7 aloud. Then read Romans 8:9 aloud. What message does Paul point to in both letters? Is it possible to be a Christian but not have the Holy Spirit? Why or why not?

8. Read Galatians 5:4 aloud. What is Paul *not* saying here? And what point is Paul aiming to convey?

9. How would you summarize the theme of the book of James? How would you summarize the theme of the book of Galatians? How is it possible that these two books work together in their message to believers?

10. What is your favorite thing you read about God's character in your God Shots from this week?

1. In Paul's missionary journeys, he uses Scripture to reason with the people in the synagogues, but when he gets to Athens, he encounters people who have no experience with Scripture. How does he shift his approach? What lessons can we take from this that will help us better engage with the world around us and share the gospel with those who don't know Jesus?

2. Compare Paul's approach to teaching different groups with the way Jesus adapted His message for different audiences. What similarities do you notice? What difference, or differences, do you notice?

3. Look back at the first part of question 2. Like Jesus, Paul often has different instructions for the way believers conduct themselves when they're around other believers versus unbelievers. Revisit Paul's words to the church at Corinth about eating meat sacrificed to idols. In what situations is that acceptable? And when it's unacceptable, what's the *reason* it's unacceptable?

4. Paul, Aquila, and Priscilla meet people in Ephesus who have been baptized in water but who don't have the Holy Spirit (Acts 18:24–19:7). How is their situation unique for their time frame?

How does it help distinguish a water baptism from the moment of salvation? (See Romans 8:9 for help.)

5. Read 1 Corinthians 1:17 aloud. Why do you think Paul steers away from baptizing people himself? What lessons can we take from this when paired with his other teachings on baptism?

6. How would you define what it means to be free in Christ? What does it mean and what does it *not* mean? How has the church at Corinth misunderstood and misapplied "freedom in Christ"?

7. Read 1 Corinthians 5:11–12 aloud. How should we go about applying Paul's instructions today? What are some ways this can be done well and ways it can be done poorly?

8. Read 1 Corinthians 10:13 aloud. In what ways has this verse been taken out of context? What does it mean, and what does it *not* mean? What is the heart of Paul's encouragement in this verse?

9. Paul's famous "love chapter" (1 Corinthians 13) falls between two chapters about spiritual gifts and how to use them. Why is love not just *helpful* but *foundational* in using our gifts?

10. What is your favorite thing you read about God's character in your God Shots from this week?

1. In 1 Corinthians 15, Paul points out that the Corinthians' disbelief in the resurrection has led them into sin and debauchery. What other foundational doctrines can you think of that, if you disbelieved them, might completely alter your lifestyle, mind-set, and actions? How can we know which doctrines should be held as absolutes versus convictions or opinions?

2. Read 2 Corinthians 3:7–10 aloud. In this section, Paul demonstrates the distinction between the old covenant (law) and the new covenant (grace). Paul describes the old covenant using words like *death* and *condemnation*, and he describes the new covenant using words like *righteousness* and *more glory*. If this is the case, why did we need the old covenant of the law at all?

3. Read 2 Corinthians 7:10 aloud. Think back on the story of Jesus's arrest and crucifixion. Which of the apostles suffered worldly grief? Which of the apostles suffered godly grief? How would you describe the difference between the two types of grief?

4. Read 2 Corinthians 13:5 aloud. What does it look like to practically apply this verse? How can we examine ourselves to see if we are in the faith?

5. In Romans 1, Paul talks about how God is righteous to judge sinners. In chapter 2, he talks about the necessity of the law. Then in chapter 3, he talks about the free gift of salvation, generously given by the grace of God, through no merit of our own. How does remembering our sin and brokenness in light of God's justice help us have a fuller understanding of the beauty of God's gift of salvation? Would you be grateful for salvation if you wrongly believed you earned it? Would you praise God for His gift if you were under the false impression that you deserved it? Why is it necessary to understand the law before we can fully understand the gospel?

6. Read Romans 4:11 aloud. Then read Galatians 3:7 and 3:29 aloud. How is Paul reframing our understanding of what it means to be in the family of faith? How does this parallel God's adoption of His children from among all the people He created?

7. How could Abraham have saving faith when Jesus hadn't even been born yet? (See Romans 4:13–25 and Hebrews 11:1–19 for help.)

8. Read Romans 8:28 aloud. What does this verse *not* mean? What does it mean?

9. What struggles (if any) did Romans 9 present for you? What other Scriptures or resources have helped you work through those struggles?

10. What is your favorite thing you read about God's character in your God Shots from this week?

1. Read Romans 11:25–26 aloud. What do you think Paul means here? What other Scriptures inform your view?

2. In Romans 13, Paul talks about submitting to authorities and fulfilling the law of love. Which aspects of this chapter are most challenging to you? Why? How can Christ's example in that specific area serve as a guide and an encouragement to you?

3. Read Romans 15:4 aloud. How have the Hebrew Scriptures given you hope? Which Old Testament stories and truths have been most impactful in strengthening your hope in God?

4. In Acts 22, the Jews are happy to hear Paul's testimony about Jesus until he mentions that this good news is for the Gentiles too. In Luke 4, Jesus experienced something similar. He had just announced to the synagogue that He was the Messiah, and they all spoke well of Him and marveled at His words in 4:22. But by 4:28, they were filled with wrath and trying to throw Him off a cliff. In between those verses, He had told them that God shows love and mercy to the Gentiles, who were their enemies. What do these two instances reveal to us about the challenges of nationalism facing the early church? Do you see any similar struggles in the church today?

5. Both Jesus and Paul take their message first to the Jews, then to the Gentiles. Why do you think they work in this order? Can you think of any Scriptures that point to the reasons behind this?

6. Read Colossians 1:24 aloud. What does this verse *not* mean? What does it mean? What other verses help us understand this verse better? (See John 19:28–30 for help.)

7. How does the story of Philemon and Onesimus remind us of the hope of God's restoration and reconciliation? What does it reveal about the power of the gospel?

8. Read Ephesians 1:11 aloud. If God works *all things* according to the counsel of His will, why do you think we tend to view some things as "too small" to pray about or seek His guidance on? What does this reveal about our view of God? What does this reveal about our view of ourselves?

9. Ephesians is Paul's first letter to the Gentiles. Read 2:18–22 aloud and reflect on this question: What phrases does Paul use to make sure they know they're included in God's family and that God dwells in them too?

10. What is your favorite thing you read about God's character in your God Shots from this week?

1. Read Philippians 2:12–13 aloud. How does the command of verse 12 rely on the truth of verse 13? What is the danger in trying to disconnect the command from its root cause and source?

2. In Paul's letters to Timothy and Titus, he repeatedly mentions rebukes. He addresses who to rebuke (1 Timothy 5:20; 2 Timothy 4:2; Titus 1:9, 1:13, 2:15) and who *not* to rebuke (1 Timothy 5:1). What are some ways rebuke can be done rightly and what are some ways it can be done wrongly? What truths about others and about ourselves are important to remember when delivering a rebuke of any kind?

3. In Paul's lists of qualifications for elders, or overseers, in 1 Timothy 3 and Titus 1, he says they must be "above reproach." What does this phrase mean? What kinds of "reproachable" things would disqualify someone from that category that aren't already mentioned elsewhere in Paul's lists? (You can review both lists in 1 Timothy 3:1–7 and Titus 1:5–9.)

4. Read 1 Peter 2:15–17 aloud. This is one of the places in Scripture where God's will for us is stated directly. What is it? Which aspect of God's will (from this list) is most challenging for you on a daily basis?

5. Read Hebrews 3:12–13 aloud. *Exhort* means "to strongly encourage or urge someone to do something." How are we practicing this in our own community? What are some other ways we might engage in this?

6. Read Hebrews 6:4–6 aloud. What parts of this passage are hard to understand or reconcile with what we know about salvation? Read 6:9–11 aloud. Does this context help you understand the way the author frames his earlier statement? (See John 6:37 and 10:28, Romans 8:38–39, Ephesians 1:13, and Philippians 1:6 for help.)

7. Why do you think the author of Hebrews continually reiterates that Christ's death was a once for all time event? What is the danger of thinking otherwise? If the readers of Hebrews at the time the letter is written are primarily Jewish, what additional doctrinal struggles might they have if they don't believe this?

8. What are some common misunderstandings about how the people in the Old Testament were saved? Why do you think it's easy to hold those views? Read Hebrews 11:1–2 aloud. How does this passage—along with the other verses referencing that Christ's death was once for all time—help resolve and clarify this issue?

9. What is your favorite thing you read about God's character in your God Shots from this week?

1. Read 2 Timothy 4:3–4 aloud. In what ways do you see this manifesting in our world today? Where do you see it in your own life? What can you do to fight against it in your own life?

2. In 2 Peter 1:17–21, Peter, who heard the audible voice of God the Father when Jesus was on earth, says there is something more sure or trustworthy than audible voices. What is it? Why is it especially important for us to esteem the written Word of God above the words of teachers and prophets and even what we believe to be God's personal direction to us?

3. Read 2 Peter 3:8 aloud. What are some ways this verse might be misinterpreted? What are some ways it might be interpreted accurately (i.e., ways that fit with the rest of Scripture)?

4. What is the commonly held view of Satan and his role in hell? Read 2 Peter 2:4 and Jude 1:6 aloud. How do these passages correct that view of Satan and his fallen angels?

5. Read 2 John 3:2 aloud. What was Jesus like when the disciples last saw Him? What hints might this text give us about our resurrection bodies?

6. Based on your current understanding of the biblical timeline, do you believe the prophecies of Revelation 11 have already happened, will happen literally, or will happen symbolically to God's people? Why?

7. In all the destruction in the book of Revelation, did you ever feel like there was a moment when God wasn't in control? Is it helpful to remember His sovereignty in these trials? Why or why not?

8. In all John's visions of beasts, the dragon, and the women, which symbol seemed most straightforward and easiest for you to connect with the story of Israel? Which one was most challenging for you to understand? Why?

9. Read Revelation 19:11–16 aloud. What stands out to you most in this description of Jesus?

10. What is your favorite thing you read about God's character in your God Shots from this week?

11. What stands out to you most from your time in this reading plan? What is your favorite thing you've learned about God?

About the Author

Tara-Leigh Cobble's zeal for biblical literacy led her to create and develop an international network of Bible studies called D-Group (Discipleship Group) International. Every week, hundreds of men's and women's D-Groups meet in homes and churches around the world to study Scripture. She also writes and hosts a daily podcast called *The Bible Recap*, designed to help listeners read and understand the Bible in a year. The podcast garnered over one hundred million downloads in its first three years, and more than twenty thousand churches around the world have joined their reading plan to know and love God better. It has been turned into a book published by Bethany House Publishers.

Tara-Leigh speaks to a wide variety of audiences, and she regularly leads teaching trips to Israel because she loves to watch others be awed by the story of Scripture through firsthand experience.

Her favorite things include sparkling water and days that are 72 degrees with 55 percent humidity. She thinks every meal tastes better when eaten outside. She lives in a concrete box in the skies of Dallas, Texas, where she has no pets, children, or anything that might die if she forgets to feed it.

For more information about Tara-Leigh and her ministries, you can visit her online.

WEBSITES:
taraleighcobble.com | thebiblerecap.com | mydgroup.org | israelux.com

SOCIAL MEDIA:
@taraleighcobble | @thebiblerecap | @mydgroup | @israeluxtours

Also from Tara-Leigh Cobble

This attractive deluxe edition of *The Bible Recap* features an imitation leather cover, a ribbon marker, and a striking two-color interior. This makes the perfect gift for holidays, celebrations, or simply encouraging someone in their faith.

The Bible Recap Deluxe

Dig deeper into the Word with *The Bible Recap Study Guide* with daily reflection and research questions specific to each day's reading and space to write your responses and notes.

The Bible Recap Study Guide

Tie your study together with *The Bible Recap Journal*, which offers writing prompts and uniquely organized space perfect for recording and tracking each day through the whole Bible.

The Bible Recap Journal

BETHANYHOUSE

 Stay up to date on your favorite books and authors with our free e-newsletters. Sign up today at bethanyhouse.com.

 facebook.com/BHPnonfiction

 @bethany_house

 @bethany_house_nonfiction

You May Also Like . . .

Popular podcast host and author Tara-Leigh Cobble offers 100 scriptural devotions to get into the Word. This easy-to-understand devotional will help you know God as you read daily snapshots of His infinite personality. Be encouraged with quick and easily understood scriptural studies, learning how to spot God shining through in your own Bible reading.

The God Shot

BETHANYHOUSE